The Greatest Lodge Cast Iron Cookbook

Simple and Easy with **Over 150 Recipes** for Your Cast-Iron Cookware

Part 3 of 4

MICHAEL FIRSTTEST

Shrimp with Fresh Basil, Thai Style

SHRIMP WITH FRESH BASIL, THAI STYLE

serves 3 to 4

This stir-fry comes from Asian cooking expert and cookbook author Nancie McDermott. She based it on the Thai dish chicken with holy basil (*gai paht bai graprao*), substituting shrimp—which, though not typical, is delicious and gorgeous— adding more onion and less chile heat, and using sweet Thai basil. It's wonderful served over rice, orzo, or couscous, or offered up with a salad or garlicky sautéed greens and good crusty bread and butter.

2	tablespoons Asian fish sauce
2	tablespoons water
1	teaspoon soy sauce
$1/2$	teaspoon sugar
2	tablespoons vegetable oil
1	pound medium shrimp, peeled and deveined
1	cup thinly sliced onion (sliced into half moons and pulled apart into strips)
1	tablespoon chopped garlic
$1/4$	cup finely chopped green onions
2	tablespoons coarsely chopped fresh cilantro
1	tablespoon seeded and chopped jalapeño, serrano, or other green chile
$3/4$	cup loosely packed fresh Thai or other basil leaves

1. Stir together the fish sauce, water, soy sauce, and sugar in a small bowl and set aside. Prep the remaining ingredients, so you can add them quickly when they are needed.

2. Place a 10-or 12-inch cast iron skillet over medium-high heat until it becomes very hot, about 30 seconds.

3. Add the oil and turn to coat the pan evenly. Add the shrimp in a single layer and leave them to cook on one side, undisturbed, until their edges turn bright pink. Toss well and turn all the shrimp cooked side up so the other side can cook, undisturbed, for 15 seconds.

4. Add the onion and garlic and toss well. Cook 1 minute, tossing occasionally, until the onion softens and becomes fragrant and shiny; continue tossing so it wilts and softens but doesn't brown.

5. Stir the fish sauce mixture to make sure the sugar is dissolved and pour it around the edge of the pan. Toss well to season the shrimp with the sauce, then let cook, undisturbed, just until the shrimp are cooked through and the sauce is bubbling. (The sauce will not be thick; it will have the consistency of thin pan juices.)

6. Add the green onions, cilantro, and chile and toss well. Tear any big basil leaves into 2 or 3 pieces each (you want to tear the basil at the very last minute, otherwise it will darken). Add all of the basil to the pan over the shrimp and toss well. Cook 10 seconds and pour onto a serving platter deep enough to hold a little sauce. Serve hot.

BLACK PEPPER SKILLET SHRIMP *(Meen Varuval)*

serves 4

In this recipe from Julie Sahni, author of the acclaimed *Classic Indian Cooking* and *Classic Indian Vegetarian and Grain Cooking*, shrimp are seared with ginger and black peppercorns. Julie suggests serving it with a green salad and sweet dinner rolls "to mop up those spicy juices" or with a fragrant rice pilaf studded with raisins.

1	pound large shrimp
2	tablespoons vegetable oil
2	tablespoons shredded peeled fresh ginger
2	teaspoons ground coriander
$1^1/_2$	teaspoons cracked black peppercorns
$^1/_2$	teaspoon sugar

Juice of $^1/_2$ lime

$^1/_2$	teaspoon kosher salt or to taste
2	tablespoons thinly sliced green onions (green part only)

1. Peel and devein the shrimp, leaving the last shell segment and tail intact.

2. Heat the oil in a 9-inch cast iron skillet over high heat until very hot, about 3 minutes. Add the ginger and cook, stirring, until it turns light brown and is caramelized, about 2 minutes. Stir in the coriander, cracked peppercorns, and sugar and let heat for 15 seconds.

3. Add the shrimp and cook, shaking and tossing, until they turn pink and curl up, about 2 minutes. Sprinkle with the lime juice, salt, and green onions. Stir gently and serve from the skillet.

Savannah Red Rice

SAVANNAH RED RICE

serves 6

This version of the classic rice dish (which is a Southern coastal interpretation of paella) is from Steven Satterfield, executive chef/owner of Miller Union in Atlanta. A few things are crucial to the final flavor of the dish. The first is using Carolina Gold rice, an heirloom variety of long-grain rice that is hand-harvested by its producer Anson Mills (buy it online at _ansonmills.com_). Sautéing the rice in fat for a good 5 minutes helps to infuse flavor into the individual grains. Lastly, no peeking while the rice is cooking—the covered cast iron pot is key to the development of the crust on the bottom. Steven likes to serve this with a green salad and roasted okra.

4   tablespoons bacon drippings

5   tablespoons butter

1   small yellow onion, diced

1   cup diced celery (inner leaves included)

2   garlic cloves, minced

2   tablespoons plus 1 teaspoon kosher salt or more to taste

2   cups canned organic whole plum tomatoes, undrained, chopped

2   cups chicken stock

2   tablespoons pepper vinegar or cider vinegar (if you use cider vinegar, add a pinch of red pepper flakes)

$1^{1}/_{4}$ teaspoons freshly ground black pepper

$^{3}/_{4}$ teaspoon dried thyme

2   bay leaves

2   dried chiles de arbol, chopped, or a pinch of red pepper flakes

2   cups long-grain rice (such as Carolina Gold)

$^{1}/_{2}$ pound andouille or chorizo sausage, grilled and sliced $^{1}/_{2}$ inch thick

1   pound shrimp, peeled, deveined, and cut into bite-size pieces

1. Heat 2 tablespoons bacon drippings and 2 tablespoons butter in a medium saucepan over medium heat until melted. Add the onion, celery, garlic, and 1 tablespoon salt; cook, stirring often, until the onion and garlic are tender. Add the tomatoes, stock, vinegar, 1 tablespoon salt, 1 teaspoon black pepper, the thyme, bay leaves, and chiles; simmer 15 to 20 minutes, tasting for seasoning.

2. Heat the remaining 2 tablespoons bacon drippings and 2 tablespoons butter in a large cast iron skillet over medium heat until foamy. Add the rice and cook, stirring frequently, until it is opaque, about 5 minutes. This step is very important to the final flavor of the dish, so don't skimp on the time—but also don't let the rice burn.

3. Add 4 cups of the tomato mixture to the rice; stir to combine, and cover. Set a timer and cook the rice for 25 minutes over very low heat. DO NOT LIFT THE LID. After 25 minutes, turn off the heat and let the rice stand for 5 more minutes. AGAIN, DO NOT LIFT THE LID. While the rice cooks, add the sausage to the remaining tomato mixture in the pan; cover and keep warm over very low heat.

4. While the rice is standing, melt the remaining 1 tablespoon butter in a medium sauté pan over medium-high heat until foamy. Add the shrimp and cook, stirring just until cooked through; add the remaining 1 teaspoon salt and $1/4$ teaspoon black pepper. Add the shrimp to the sausage and tomato mixture, and stir well.

5. Pour the shrimp and sausage mixture over the rice. Remove and discard bay leaves. Gently fluff the rice (you don't want to break the grains) to combine. Serve immediately.

BARBECUE SHRIMP OVER RICE

serves 8

It's risky to use the word "barbecue" in the South because it means a wide range of things overall, and yet a very specific thing to each individual. In this recipe, from Sheri Castle, a food writer and cooking teacher in Chapel Hill, North Carolina, succulent shrimp are seared in a sensational barbecue sauce in a hot cast iron skillet. The high heat quickly cooks the shrimp and produces a spicy, buttery, lemony sauce to spoon over hot rice. The ingredient list looks long, but the recipe comes together quickly and relies mostly on pantry staples. Be sure to use jumbo or extra-large shrimp that will not overcook and turn rubbery.

2/3 cup tomato sauce

2/3 cup ketchup

1/3 cup unfiltered cider vinegar

1/4 cup firmly packed light brown sugar

2 tablespoons Worcestershire sauce

1 teaspoon garlic powder

1 teaspoon onion powder

2 teaspoons cracked or coarsely ground black pepper

1 teaspoon salt

1 teaspoon sweet paprika

1 teaspoon smoked paprika

1 teaspoon dried basil

1 teaspoon dried oregano

1 teaspoon dried thyme

1/4 teaspoon cayenne pepper or to taste

2 1/2 to 3 pounds extra-jumbo shrimp (16 to 20), peeled and deveined

1/2 cup fresh lemon juice

1/2 cup (1 stick) butter, cut into small pieces

Hot cooked long-grain rice

1. Stir together the first 15 ingredients in a large bowl. Add the shrimp and toss to coat.

2. Heat a large cast iron skillet (preferably large enough to hold the shrimp in a single layer) over high heat until very hot. Carefully pour

in the shrimp and sauce. (Watch out for spatters!) The liquid should boil and hiss.

3. Cook, stirring well and scraping the sauce from the bottom of the skillet, until the shrimp begin to turn pink and the sauce thickens, depending on size of the shrimp, about 2 minutes. Remove the skillet from the heat and add the lemon juice and butter. Stir until the butter melts and the shrimp are cooked through.

4. Serve immediately over plenty of hot rice to soak up the delicious sauce.

SCALLOP PIE

serves 2 to 4

Janene White of Sacramento, California, offers this rich and creamy traditional Irish meal to fellow scallop lovers. Enjoy it as a main dish served with some astringent field greens or asparagus as a counterpoint. Or for the ultimate decadent surf-and-turf, serve it with your favorite steak dinner.

½   cup milk
1   bay leaf
1   pound scallops
Salt and freshly ground black pepper
½   cup heavy cream
2   cups finely chopped yellow onion
4   tablespoons butter
2   tablespoons all-purpose flour
1   garlic clove, crushed into a paste
½   tablespoon Irish whiskey
4   ounces mushrooms, sliced
½   cup fine, dry breadcrumbs

1. Bring the milk and bay leaf to a simmer in a 10-inch cast iron skillet over medium heat. Add the scallops and season with salt and pepper to taste. Cook the scallops until they are opaque all the way through, about 5 minutes; remove them from the pan with a slotted spoon. If you're using sea scallops, cut each one into quarters when they're cool enough to handle. Pour the cream into a small bowl; pour the milk mixture through a fine wire-mesh strainer into the cream, discard the solids, and set aside. Wipe the skillet clean.

2. Preheat the broiler.

3. Add the onion to the skillet and cook over medium heat, stirring occasionally, until just softened. Add 2 tablespoons butter, stirring to melt, then sprinkle in the flour; stir continually for about 1 minute. (Don't overstir or the mixture will become pasty.) Slowly pour in the milk and cream mixture, stirring constantly. Continue to stir until sauce is smooth. Stir in the garlic and whiskey and simmer 5 minutes. Stir in the scallops and mushrooms.

4. Sprinkle the top with the breadcrumbs. Cut the remaining 2 tablespoons butter into small pieces and sprinkle over the crumbs. Place under the broiler until the top is browned.

Variation: Instead of breadcrumbs, you can spread mashed potatoes over the top. Sprinkle with the butter and bake at 350° until the top browns, about 20 minutes.

Casserole of Scallops, Chestnut Farro, and Hen
of the Woods Mushrooms with Sorghum Veal Glacé

CASSEROLE OF SCALLOPS, CHESTNUT FARRO, AND HEN OF THE WOODS MUSHROOMS WITH SORGHUM VEAL GLACÉ

serves 4

This recipe comes from Linton Hopkins, chef/owner of Restaurant Eugene and Holeman & Finch Public House in Atlanta.

Chestnut Farro:

$^1/_2$ cup farro (Linton uses Anson Mills brand)

$2^1/_2$ cups chicken stock

1 bay leaf

1 teaspoon salt, plus more to taste

2 tablespoons unsalted butter

1 tablespoon minced jarred chestnuts

3 tablespoons minced shallots

1 tablespoon minced celery

$^1/_2$ teaspoon minced garlic

1 tablespoon minced fresh flat-leaf parsley

Grated zest and juice of 1 lemon

Freshly ground black pepper

Mushrooms:

1 pound hen of the woods (maitake) or shiitake mushrooms

3 tablespoons extra-virgin olive oil

Salt

1 cup chicken stock

1 teaspoon chopped fresh flat-leaf parsley

1 teaspoon unsalted butter

Freshly ground black pepper

Bacon:

2   ounces smoked slab bacon (Linton prefers Benton's)

Sorghum Veal Glacé:

4   teaspoons reduced veal stock or store-bought veal demi-glacé

1   teaspoon sorghum syrup

Scallops:

8   jumbo sea scallops

Salt

2   tablespoons peanut oil

1. Make the farro: Combine the farro, chicken stock, bay leaf, and salt in a medium saucepan; bring to a boil, reduce the heat, and simmer until farro is tender, about 2 hours. Remove from the heat.

2. Melt the butter in a medium cast iron skillet over medium heat until foamy. Add the chestnuts and toast. Add the shallots, celery, and garlic and cook, stirring occasionally, until the shallots are translucent. Add the farro to the skillet along with any liquid still in the saucepan. Stir in the parsley and lemon zest and juice; season with salt and pepper to taste; cover and keep warm.

3. Prepare the mushrooms: Preheat the oven to 350°. Break the mushrooms into smaller pieces (if using shiitakes, discard the stems). Place the mushrooms, olive oil, and salt to taste in a large cast iron skillet. Place the skillet in the oven and roast until the mushrooms are browned and tender, about 7 minutes.

4. Place the skillet over high heat. Add the chicken stock to the skillet and bring to a boil; reduce the stock to a glaze. Add the parsley and butter; stir until the butter melts. Season with salt and pepper to taste; cover and keep warm.

5. Cut the bacon into 4 cubes. Place the cubes in a small cast iron skillet over medium heat and cook until golden brown on all sides. Remove to a paper towel to drain.

6. Make the sorghum veal glacé: Combine the veal stock and sorghum

syrup in a small saucepan and cook until hot. Keep warm.

7. Season the scallops with salt to taste. Heat the peanut oil in a medium cast iron skillet over high heat until hot. Sear the scallops on both sides until golden brown and just cooked through.

8. To serve, spoon some of the farro mixture into each of 4 individual Lodge Oblong Mini Servers. Top with a bacon cube, some of the mushroom mixture, and 2 of the scallops. Drizzle the glacé over each serving and serve immediately.

MOTHER'S FAVORITE FRIED CHICKEN

serves 5 to 6

When Billie Cline Hill was a small child in the 1930s, her parents, Kate Belk and John Douglas Cline, opened a grocery store on Cedar Avenue in South Pittsburg, Tennessee. Mrs. Cline would cook the family meals in the rear of the store. Workmen at the Sequachee Valley Electric Cooperative building next door had a break at 9 a.m., and Billie's mother always put out a plate of leftovers from the previous night's dinner for the men to enjoy. Her fried chicken was such a favorite that she always cooked extra just for them.

1   cup all-purpose flour

1   tablespoon salt

1   teaspoon freshly ground black pepper

2   cups vegetable shortening

2   large eggs

$^1/_4$ cup milk

1   whole chicken, cut into 8 pieces

1. Combine the flour, salt, and pepper in a bowl large enough to hold the largest piece of chicken.

2. Heat the shortening in a large cast iron Dutch oven or the fryer of a Lodge Combo Cooker over medium heat to 325°.

3. While the shortening heats, beat the eggs and milk in a bowl large enough to hold the largest piece of chicken. Dip the chicken pieces, one at a time, into the egg mixture, dredge them in the flour mixture, and then back into the egg mixture and the flour mixture.

4. Slowly fry the chicken until it is golden brown on all sides and cooked through. You may need to turn the heat down to prevent the chicken from getting too brown before it's done.

SPATCHCOCK CHICKEN

serves 2

This simple dish comes from Patrick Reilly of the Majestic Grille in Memphis. The hardest part is deboning the chicken, but it is so worth the effort. You can do it yourself, or ask your butcher to do it for you. Make sure you save the bones and wings—they make the best chicken stock ever. Patrick likes to serve this with a tomato salad and <u>Lyonnaise Potatoes</u>.

1 (3-pound) fryer chicken (look for a farm-raised organic bird—Patrick loves West Wind Farms from Deer Lodge, Tennessee)

1 tablespoon olive oil

Kosher salt and freshly ground black pepper

1. To debone the chicken, place the chicken on a cutting board, breast side up, with the legs pointing away from you. With a sharp knife, cut down the left center of the breast, keeping the tip of the knife along the edge of the breastbone, until you have cut the bird in half. Cut through the wing joint where it connects to the breast. Turn the chicken on its side and gently pull the leg back toward the breast until the leg joint pops out. Cut around the leg, removing the leg and the breast in one piece. Repeat with the other half of the chicken. Cut a slit down the length of the two bones in the legs; remove the bones, scraping the meat off as you go. Rub the chicken with the oil and season with salt and pepper to taste.

2. Heat a large cast iron grill pan over medium heat. Place the two chicken halves, skin side up, in the pan, and cook 8 minutes. Flip the chicken over, place a cast iron grill press on top, and cook until the juices run clear and the skin has turned golden brown and crispy, about 10 minutes. Let the chicken rest a few minutes. You can either serve each diner half a chicken or carve it into thick slices.

NONA'S CHICKEN

serves 6

This recipe comes from cookbook author Diane Phillips's grandmother, Aleandra Ciuffoli Pasquini. Although her Nona used red wine vinegar, Diane prefers the sweeter flavor of good aged balsamic vinegar. Serve the chicken over sautéed potatoes like Nona did.

6   thick bacon slices, cut into $\frac{1}{2}$-inch pieces

$\frac{1}{4}$ cup olive oil, if needed (see <u>Note</u>)

1   (3-pound) whole chicken, cut into 8 pieces

2   teaspoons salt

1   teaspoon freshly ground black pepper

4   garlic cloves, sliced

2   tablespoons fresh rosemary leaves, finely chopped

$\frac{1}{4}$ cup balsamic vinegar

1. Cook the bacon in a 12-inch cast iron skillet over medium-high heat, stirring often, until crisp. Add as much of the oil to the bacon and drippings in the pan as needed before adding the chicken (see <u>Note</u>).

2. While the bacon cooks, sprinkle the chicken pieces evenly with the salt and pepper. Add the chicken to the skillet and brown over medium-high heat on all sides, turning when each side is browned. While the chicken is browning, add the garlic and rosemary. When the chicken is browned, add the vinegar and turn the pieces of chicken to coat them with it.

3. Cover the skillet and cook over medium-high heat until a meat thermometer inserted into the thickest portion registers 165° and the chicken is cooked through, about 10 minutes.

{ note }

If the bacon is quite lean, there will not be enough fat in the pan to brown the chicken; add as much of the olive oil to the pan as you think necessary before adding the chicken.

Sizzling bacon pieces hopped in the coal black skillet as Nona would gently cook it until crispy. When the bacon was crisp, she would add the chicken pieces, cut up and sprinkled liberally with salt and pepper, spitting and tossing up steam when they hit the pan. As the aromas rose from the skillet, Nona would slice several cloves of garlic and drop them in. Hearing the sizzle, she would grunt, turn to the fresh rosemary on the counter, and begin to chop. The pan was taking care of her ingredients; she knew that the chicken would release from the pan once it was browned, almost like a modern-day nonstick pan. The rosemary was tossed in, the chicken turned again, and then red wine vinegar was added. The hiss and bubble of the pan juices would erupt into a fog of garlic-rosemary aroma. Once the chicken was cooked, it was transferred to a platter and covered with aluminum foil.

If you were quite clever, you could sneak just a bit of chicken to taste or a scrap of bacon. Once the pan was free, more bacon fat went in, as well as diced potatoes. Sprinkled with salt and pepper and tossed in the fat, the potatoes turned translucent, then slowly golden, and then crusty brown, turned constantly to give them an even, crunchy crust. The chicken was arranged over the potatoes, its sauce spooned over everything. The coal black pan cooled to room temperature and was carefully cleaned, and then put back on the stove-top to dry and season.

Nona's skillet reminded her of Italy, the land she'd left as an 18-year-old with two children to come to a foreign country and make a home, without her extended family or the ingredients she knew. That skillet was her tie to Umbria; it was similar to those her mother had used and enabled her to make the dishes she remembered with love and longing.

The skillet made its way to my mother's house after Nona died; she would cook her chicken just as Nona had and make sure to carefully dry and reseason the pan before putting it away. And when she passed on, it came to me.   —Diane Phillips

Grilled Chicken with Citrus Salsa

GRILLED CHICKEN WITH CITRUS SALSA

serves 4

A resident of South Pittsburg, Tennessee, Wayne Gray, with his horse, Lady, participates in Civil War reenactments as an East Tennessee Federalist.

1   jalapeño chile, sliced
$1/4$ cup plus 1 tablespoon fresh lime juice
$1/4$ cup plus 1 tablespoon olive oil
4   skinned and boned chicken breasts
Salt and freshly ground black pepper
1   navel orange, sectioned and cut into $1/4$-inch pieces
1   small grapefruit, sectioned and cut into $1/4$-inch pieces
4   green onions, thinly sliced
10 cherry tomatoes, seeded and diced
Grated zest of $1/2$ orange
Grated zest of $1/2$ lime
1   jalapeño chile, minced
4   handfuls mixed greens

1. Combine the jalapeño slices with $1/4$ cup each of the lime juice and oil in a shallow bowl.

2. Rub the chicken with salt and pepper to taste and place in the jalapeño marinade, turning to coat both sides. Cover and refrigerate 30 minutes.

3. Combine the orange and grapefruit pieces, green onions, tomatoes, orange and lime zest, minced jalapeño, the remaining 1 tablespoon each lime juice and oil, and salt and pepper to taste. Set salsa aside.

4. Remove the chicken from the marinade; discard the marinade. Grease a 10-inch cast iron grill pan and heat over medium-high heat

until hot. Add the chicken and cook 5 minutes on each side, until done. Remove the cooked chicken from the pan and let stand 5 minutes.

5. Divide the greens among 4 serving plates. Slice each chicken breast and place over the greens on each plate. Spoon the salsa over the top and serve immediately.

a cast iron memory

I love the South. I love the way we sit on porches and wave to whoever passes, whether we know them or not. And the way men wave to one another in their pickup trucks, raising their index finger without removing their hand from the steering wheel. And I love the way our mothers hand down recipes and their black-as-pitch cast iron skillets like they were passing down a country estate. The best recipes ("Simply the best, I tell you, darlin'") are passed along in a bit of a whisper while sitting on the front porch, like they contained "11 herbs and spices" otherwise kept in a vault. That's how this recipe came to me and my wife, Ann, whispered between waves to strangers while sitting on a porch. It's the best, darlin'. Trust me.   —Wayne Gray

SMOTHERED CHICKEN WITH BUTTER BEANS

serves 6

Chef John D. Folse's grandfather grew beans of every variety in his garden on Cabanocey Plantation. "I vividly remember the eight Folse children circling a large washtub to shell the fresh beans," recalls Chef Folse, who is the founder and namesake of the John Folse Culinary Institute at Nicholls State University in Thibodaux, Louisiana. "They went into everything from shrimp dishes to casseroles, including this preparation, one of my grandfather's favorites." Serve it over steamed white rice. This recipe comes from Chef Folse's cookbook *The Encyclopedia of Cajun & Creole Cuisine*.

$\frac{1}{4}$ cup vegetable oil

¼   cup all-purpose flour

1   cup diced onion

1   cup diced red bell pepper

¼   cup minced garlic

1   (3-pound) fryer chicken, cut into 8 pieces

3   cups chicken stock, or as needed

4   cups shelled fresh butter beans

Salt and freshly ground black pepper

½   cup sliced green onions

1. Heat the oil in a large cast iron Dutch oven over medium-high heat. Slowly whisk in the flour and stir constantly until you have a light brown roux (it should be the color of peanut butter).

2. Add the onion, bell pepper, and garlic, and cook, stirring frequently, until the vegetables are wilted. Add the chicken and cook until well browned on all sides, 5 to 10 minutes. Add the stock and stir well; you may need to add more stock or water to achieve a stew-like consistency. Add the butter beans and season with salt and pepper to taste. Bring to a rolling boil; reduce the heat and simmer until the chicken is cooked through and tender, 30 to 45 minutes.

3. Stir in the green onions; taste and adjust the seasoning, if desired.

STUFFED GARLIC CHICKEN BREASTS

serves 4

You get a double hit of garlic in this dish—in the chicken's creamy filling and in the sauce that tops it. This recipe was contributed by International Dutch Oven Society member E.T. Moore.

4   ounces cream cheese, softened

4   garlic cloves, chopped

1   large onion, chopped
¼   teaspoon red pepper flakes
4   skinned and boned chicken breast halves
Salt and freshly ground black pepper
2   tablespoons canola oil
¼   cup (½ stick) salted butter
2   tablespoons white or cider vinegar
2   tablespoons barbecue sauce of your choice
⅓   cup (1½ ounces) shredded Parmesan cheese

1. Preheat the oven to 350°.

2. Combine the cream cheese, ¾ of the garlic and onion, and the red pepper in a medium bowl. Mix well.

3. Cutting into a long side of each chicken breast half, slice it almost in half. Open each breast up like a book and spread ¼ of the cream cheese mixture over one side. Fold the other side of the breast over it and secure the opening with wooden picks. Season both sides of each stuffed breast with salt and black pepper to taste.

4. Heat the oil in a 12-inch cast iron skillet or large Dutch oven over medium heat. Add the chicken and sear each side 3 to 4 minutes. Transfer to oven; cover and bake for 25 minutes.

5. Meanwhile, in an 8-inch cast iron skillet, melt the butter over medium heat. Add the remaining garlic and onion and cook, stirring often, until almost soft and translucent. Add the vinegar and barbecue sauce, stir well, and heat through.

6. Remove the skillet from the oven and pour the sauce over the chicken. Sprinkle the Parmesan over the chicken. Return the chicken to the oven and bake, covered, until done, another 10 to 15 minutes.

Chicken with Artichoke Hearts, Olives, and Capers

CHICKEN WITH ARTICHOKE HEARTS, OLIVES, AND CAPERS

serves 4

Cookbook author and *Bon Appétit* contributing editor Dede Wilson has made this with both boneless, skinless thighs as well as breasts. You can also substitute white wine for the red for a slightly less dark and rich dish. Serve it with rice or steamed potatoes—or, better yet, the next day with crusty bread.

8   skinned and boned chicken thighs or 2 skinned and boned chicken breasts (cut breasts into halves, and then cut in half crosswise)

Salt and freshly ground black pepper

2   tablespoons olive oil

1   large yellow or white onion, chopped

6   garlic cloves, minced

1   teaspoon fresh thyme leaves, crushed

$^3/_4$ cup dry red wine

1   (28-ounce) can diced tomatoes, undrained

2   tablespoons balsamic vinegar

1   (9-ounce) package frozen artichoke hearts, thawed

$^1/_4$ cup pitted green olives, such as Greek or French in brine, cut in half

$^1/_4$ cup pitted black olives, such as kalamata, cut in half

2   tablespoons drained capers

$^1/_4$ cup chopped fresh flat-leaf parsley

1. Season the chicken with salt and pepper to taste. Heat the oil in a 5-quart cast iron Dutch oven over medium-high heat. Brown chicken, a few pieces at a time, 4 minutes total for each batch (2 minutes for breasts). Remove browned chicken pieces to a platter.

2. Add the onion and cook, stirring occasionally, over medium-low heat until translucent and beginning to lightly brown, about 4 minutes. Add the garlic and thyme and cook 1 minute. Add the wine and bring to a boil, scraping the bottom of the pan to loosen browned bits and incorporate them into the liquid. Stir in the tomatoes and vinegar.

3. Return the chicken to the pan and add the artichokes, both kinds of olives, and the capers. Cover and simmer over medium-low heat until the chicken is done, about 30 minutes. Sprinkle with the parsley and serve.

Tom's Widely Known Wayfarer Chicken Curry

TOM'S WIDELY KNOWN WAYFARER CHICKEN CURRY

serves 6 to 8

Peter Gerety offers up this recipe in remembrance of his brother-in-law, Tom Hill. When they were both actors (along with Peter's sister, Anne Gerety), they ended up in Portland, Oregon, running the Storefront Theater. In order to support themselves, Tom bought a macrobiotic restaurant, called the Wayfarer. He turned it into a curry house where they all worked, when not on stage, preparing the dishes Tom grew up with in India. Serve this curry over Tom's Pulao.

2   tablespoons canola oil

2   heaping tablespoons Tom's Curry Powder

1   tablespoon chopped peeled fresh ginger

2   medium onions, chopped

3   medium tomatoes, chopped (reserve the juices)

Salt

1/2   cup canned unsweetened coconut milk

8   skin-on, bone-in chicken thighs

1. Heat the oil in a large cast iron Dutch oven over medium heat until hot. Add Tom's Curry Powder and ginger; sauté just until they release their fragrances, about 1 minute or less.

2. Add the onions, stir, and let cook until softened. Add the tomatoes and their juices and salt to taste (you can also add a little water if the tomatoes aren't juicy enough). Reduce the heat to low and simmer, uncovered, 1 hour.

3. Stir in the coconut milk. Add the chicken, turning to coat the pieces with the sauce. Bring the curry to a boil; cover, reduce the heat to medium-low, and simmer until the chicken is done, about 1 hour.

Salmon Curry: Substitute 6 to 8 (6-ounce) pieces of salmon fillet for the chicken and simmer the salmon to desired degree of doneness, about 25 minutes.

TOM'S CURRY POWDER

makes a generous ¹/₄ cup

4   teaspoons turmeric
4   teaspoons ground cumin
4   teaspoons ground coriander
1   teaspoon crushed fenugreek seeds
1   teaspoon cayenne pepper or more to taste

1. Stir together the spices in a small bowl. Store in an airtight container.

TOM'S PULAO

serves 4

A benefit to cooking rice in cast iron is that it keeps the cooked rice hot for a long time.

¹/₄   cup (¹/₂ stick) butter
1   cinnamon stick
1   bay leaf
1   teaspoon whole cloves
4   or 5 cardamom pods
¹/₂   cup raisins
2   cups rice
4   cups water
Toppings: slivered almonds, browned onion slivers, golden raisins,

unsweetened grated coconut, and/or dry-roasted peanuts

1. Melt the butter in a medium cast iron Dutch oven over medium heat. Add the cinnamon stick and next 4 ingredients; sauté 1 minute, until the spices release their fragrances. Stir to coat the raisins with the spiced butter.

2. Add the rice and stir 1 minute to coat with the spiced butter. Add the water and bring to a boil. Cover tightly, reduce the heat to the lowest setting, and cook 15 minutes.

3. Turn off the heat and let the rice steam 45 minutes (do not lift the lid during this time). Remove and discard cinnamon stick and bay leaf. Serve with the toppings.

CHICKEN TAGINE

serves 4

This is an adaptation of a recipe that originally ran in *Coastal Living* magazine. Senior Food Editor Julia Rutland has changed it up to make it a little easier and healthier. "My kids really like breast meat, so instead of a whole chicken cut into pieces, I opted for four bone-in breasts. To save time and to lighten it, I used skinless chicken. If you prefer to use skin-on chicken, brown it first in about two tablespoons olive oil," says Julia. If you see Moroccan spice blend in the store, buy that rather than having to purchase four individual spices to rub on the chicken. And if you can't find preserved lemons, substitute the juice and grated zest of a fresh lemon, and season the dish with a little more salt.

2	teaspoons ground ginger
1	teaspoon ground coriander
1	teaspoon turmeric
1	teaspoon ground cinnamon
4	skinned, bone-in chicken breasts

2 tablespoons olive oil

1 onion, thinly sliced into half moons and pulled apart into strips

4 garlic cloves, chopped

Salt and freshly ground black pepper

2 fresh parsley sprigs

2 fresh cilantro sprigs

$^{3}/_{4}$ cup water

Pinch of saffron threads

$^{1}/_{2}$ cup pitted Moroccan purple or kalamata olives

2 wedges preserved lemon, cut into thin strips

Hot cooked couscous

1. Combine the ginger, coriander, turmeric, and cinnamon in a small bowl. Sprinkle evenly on the chicken; cover and refrigerate until ready to cook.

2. Heat the oil in a large cast iron Dutch oven over medium-high heat. Add the onion and garlic and cook, stirring occasionally, until tender and just starting to brown, about 3 minutes. Add the chicken and sprinkle with salt and pepper to taste; top with the parsley and cilantro sprigs.

3. Combine the water and saffron; pour over the chicken. Bring to a boil. Cover, reduce heat, and simmer 15 minutes; stir and cook until the chicken is done, about another 15 minutes.

4. Stir in the olives and preserved lemon; cook 5 minutes, until heated. Serve with hot couscous.

TENNESSEE VALLEY JAMBALAYA

serves 6

John Richard "Dick" Lodge, Jr., likes to serve this jambalaya with hot sauce, country-style bread, and a green salad. Dick based his recipe on several jambalaya recipes, none of them particularly authentic from a Louisianan's perspective. "It is called 'Tennessee Valley' because we live in the Valley, and because country ham is included for flavor, rather than andouille or another spicy Cajun sausage," explains Dick. This was a nod to the young Lodge children, who did not like the heat of more authentic Louisiana jambalaya.

1	small whole chicken
8	links sweet or hot Italian sausage
1	cup chopped onion
1	cup chopped green bell pepper
2	to 4 garlic cloves, minced
3	tablespoons olive oil
1	cup diced country ham
1	(16-ounce) can whole tomatoes, undrained
1	cup long-grain rice
$1/2$	teaspoon dried thyme
$1/2$	to 1 teaspoon chili powder
$1^1/_2$	teaspoons salt
$1/2$	teaspoon freshly ground black pepper
$1^1/_2$	tablespoons chopped fresh parsley

1. Place the chicken in a large saucepan and cover with water. Bring to a boil, reduce the heat to a simmer, and cook until the chicken is done, about 30 minutes. Drain, reserving $1^1/_2$ cups of the broth.

2. Let the chicken stand until cool enough to handle; remove the meat from the bones and tear or cut it into bite-size pieces. Set aside.

3. While the chicken cools, place the sausage on a baking sheet and bake in a preheated 350° oven until browned and cooked through, about 30 minutes. Let stand until cool enough to handle, and then cut into $1/8$-inch-thick slices. Leave the oven on.

5. In a 5-quart cast iron Dutch oven, cook the onion, bell pepper, and

garlic in the oil over medium-high heat, stirring, just until tender. Add the chicken, sausage, ham, tomatoes, rice, reserved broth, thyme, chili powder, salt, and pepper. Bring to a boil, stirring once or twice. Cover tightly and bake for 1 hour. If the rice is still slightly crunchy, stir and bake 10 to 15 minutes longer.

6. Stir in the parsley and serve.

SEARED TEAL BREASTS

serves 4

Wild duck can be a little tricky to prepare, but Paul McIlhenny, a game cook, knows that simplicity is often the best solution. "The reason I like this recipe so well is that it doesn't totally hide the flavor of the wild duck," Paul says. "The sauce is full, without being overpowering, and complements the richness of the bird." And it's quick and easy, which makes it even better.

1/4   cup Lea & Perrins Worcestershire sauce

1   teaspoon Tabasco sauce

Cracked black peppercorns

8   skin-on boneless teal breasts, plucked clean

2   tablespoons unsalted butter

Salt

1. Combine the Worcestershire, Tabasco, and cracked peppercorns to taste in a large shallow baking dish. Add the teal breasts, turning to coat both sides in the marinade. Refrigerate 2 hours.

2. Drain the teal breasts and pat dry. Heat a large cast iron skillet over medium-high heat until hot. Add the butter, followed quickly by the teal breasts, 4 at a time, skin side down; sear 4 minutes. Turn the breasts and sear the meat side for 2 minutes; the breasts should be cooked to no more than medium rare. Transfer breasts to a cutting board and let stand 5 minutes. Repeat cooking process with the remaining teal breasts.

3. Slice each breast, across the grain, into 4 pieces, and place 2 breasts on each plate. Lightly season with salt and additional cracked pepper to taste; serve immediately.

SAGE AND CITRUS-BRAISED DUCK

serves 4 to 6

This recipe comes from environmental scientist Dr. Geraldine McGuire. Based in Queensland, Australia, she has worked with clients throughout Asia and the Pacific to blend sustainable economic, environmental, and social solutions. Also recognized as an excellent cook, she recommends serving this dish with a steamed green vegetable and potatoes fried in some of the fat you render when you sear the duck.

2   free-range ducks

1   tablespoon olive oil

3   pink grapefruit

2   oranges

1   teaspoon dried or chopped fresh sage

$1/4$ teaspoon freshly ground white pepper

Sea salt

1. Remove the breasts and legs from the ducks (discard the wings and carcasses or use them to make stock). Score the skin.

2. Heat the oil in a large cast iron skillet over medium heat. Add the duck pieces, skin side down, and sear until well browned. Turn over and brown the other side. Transfer the duck pieces to a large cast iron Dutch oven. When the drippings cool, strain the duck fat from the skillet; store the fat in the refrigerator or freezer—it adds wonderful flavor when frying potatoes.

3. Juice 2 of the grapefruit and 1 of the oranges; pour the juices over the duck pieces. Peel and cut the remaining grapefruit and orange into pieces, removing any seeds; place the pieces over the duck. Sprinkle with the sage, pepper, and salt to taste.

4. Cover the pan and cook over low heat until the duck starts to fall apart and is tender, 2 to 3 hours.

Duck Breast with Sugar Snap Peas and Mushrooms

DUCK BREAST WITH SUGAR SNAP PEAS AND MUSHROOMS

serves 4

Duck breast is a treat to enjoy at fine restaurants, but many people are hesitant to try it themselves at home. This recipe from Al Hernandez, food and wine editor of *The Vine Times*, helps you bring that tasty and elegant meal home.

4   (6-to 8-ounce) duck breasts

Salt and freshly ground black pepper

4   garlic cloves, finely chopped

¾   pound sugar snap peas, ends trimmed

8   ounces mushrooms (cremini and button mushrooms preferred), thinly sliced

2   teaspoons sherry vinegar or red wine vinegar

1. Remove any silverskin from the duck breasts and pat dry with a paper towel. Score the duck skin approximately ½ inch apart in a crisscross pattern (be sure not to cut into the duck meat). Season both sides with salt and pepper to taste.

2. Heat a large cast iron skillet over medium heat. Place the duck breasts in the hot skillet, fat side down, and sear until golden brown, 7 to 9 minutes. Turn the breasts over and cook another 5 to 7 minutes. (The recommended serving temperature for duck is 145° for medium rare.)

3. Transfer the breasts to a plate. Pour the rendered duck fat into a heatproof container; measure 1½ tablespoons of the rendered duck fat back into the skillet (refrigerate any remaining fat and use it to cook potatoes). Add the garlic, sugar snap peas, and mushrooms to the skillet. Season with salt and pepper to taste. Add the vinegar and cook, stirring, over medium heat until heated through, 5 to 7 minutes.

4. Cut the duck breasts into ½-inch-thick slices. Serve the duck with the vegetables on the side.

This remembrance and the following three recipes were contributed by J. Wayne Fears. In his wide and varied career, he has been a wildlife specialist, developed and operated hunting lodges in Alabama, and served as the editor-in-chief of *Rural Sportsman* and *Hunting Camp Journal*.

Wayne is the author of more than 25 books on outdoor-related topics and a columnist and contributor to numerous outdoor-

and hunting-related periodicals. More information can be found at his Web site, jwaynefears.com.

◇◇

CAST IRON AND COUNTRY COOKING

Growing up on the side of one of the Cumberland Mountains in North Alabama, life was simple. My dad was a trapper, and we somewhat lived off the land. The one inspiring thing about that simple lifestyle was that my mom was a master at turning anything we brought in from the woods into delicious table fare.

When I was a youngster, it was a contest up and down the valley to see who could get the circuit preacher to have Sunday dinner at their house. He preached in the valley only twice a month, and it was bragging rights to the housewife whose cooking could keep the reverend coming back to that home for encore meals. My mom found out the reverend loved fried young groundhog, and she became a repeat winner. It was great for me since I was sent out to harvest "just the right groundhog," a chore I loved.

CAST IRON INDOORS AND OUT

My mom's cookware was, by our standards, "the best money could buy"—a cast iron skillet and a couple of flat-bottomed cast iron Dutch ovens. They were handed down to her from her mom, who got them from her mother, and now, many years later, they are doing service in my kitchen and still working their cast iron magic. They are treasured heirlooms that my children look forward to getting.

As I was growing up, I accompanied my dad on many outdoor expeditions, and his camp cook kit was comprised of a cast iron skillet and a 10-inch camp Dutch oven. His dishes, prepared over an open fire next to some remote creek, instilled in me the desire to be a lifetime student of cast iron cooking. I learned early that my dad's cast iron cookware was made by a company named Lodge, and over the years I came to trust the Lodge brand in remote camps over much of the globe. Whether cooking for hunting clients over a little willow and alder fire on the headwaters of the Canning River in the Brooks Range of Alaska, or in a bean hole (see _Bean Hole Cooking_) in a remote fishing camp in the Colorado high country, or in a modern kitchen at Stagshead Lodge in Alabama, Lodge and its magic skillets and pots have produced dishes that have graced my magazine articles and books for more than four decades. The same dishes cooked in anything other than cast iron just aren't the same. As I said, there is magic in those black pots and skillets.

You try it for yourself, and you will see the difference. Here are some starter recipes featuring meats from the wild harvest.

SKILLET FRIED RABBIT WITH GRAVY

serves 4

This is a recipe I learned from George Prechter, one of New Orleans' master game chefs and a camp cook without equal. He has served this rabbit dish to many who professed how much they disliked wild game while dipping into the pan for second and third helpings.

Rabbit:

$^1/_2$ cup all-purpose flour

1   teaspoon salt

$^1/_4$ teaspoon freshly ground black pepper

1   ($2^1/_4$- to $2^3/_4$-pound) rabbit, cut into pieces

$^1/_2$ cup (1 stick) salted butter

Gravy:

3   tablespoons all-purpose flour

1   cup chicken broth

1   cup milk

$^1/_2$ teaspoon salt

$^1/_8$ teaspoon freshly ground black pepper

$\frac{1}{8}$ teaspoon dried   thyme

$\frac{1}{8}$ teaspoon dried marjoram

1. Make the rabbit: Combine the flour, salt, and pepper in a large plastic or paper bag. Dredge the rabbit pieces by shaking them in the bag. Tap off any extra flour.

2. Melt the butter in a large cast iron skillet with a lid over medium heat; add the rabbit and cook until evenly browned on all sides, 5 to 6 minutes.

3. Cover, reduce the heat to low, and cook until the rabbit is fork-tender, about 1 hour, turning 2 or 3 times. Transfer the rabbit to a serving dish and keep warm.

4. Make the gravy: Blend the flour into the pan drippings, but do not brown. Add the broth, milk, and remaining ingredients. Cook over medium heat, stirring often, until thickened. Pour the gravy over the rabbit and serve.

Tender Venison Roast

TENDER VENISON ROAST

TENDER VENISON ROAST

serves 8 to 10

I discovered this recipe back when I owned hunting lodges and served meals to dozens of guests each day. Often hunters complained of venison roast being tough and dry. Using a cast iron Dutch oven, this recipe can reliably take a less-than-tender roast, whether venison or beef, and make it fork-tender.

1   (4-pound) venison or beef roast
1   cup plus 2 teaspoons hot water
1   (1-ounce) envelope dry onion soup mix (such as Lipton)
1   tablespoon Worcestershire sauce

1. Preheat the oven to 300°.

2. Place the roast in a 12-inch cast iron Dutch oven on a small wire rack. Add 1 cup water.

3. Make a paste with the soup mix and remaining 2 teaspoons water. Brush paste over roast; sprinkle with the Worcestershire.

4. Cover the pan and bake until the roast is fork-tender, about 3 hours.

BRAISED BREAST OF GROUSE

serves 2

If ruffed grouse weighed 30 pounds, I would never hunt big game again. In my opinion, grouse is the most flavorful game bird and top table fare of all the wild harvest. Here is a recipe that, when coupled with the cast iron skillet, ensures your grouse breast of being all it can be. The recipe also works well for pheasant.

$^1/_2$ cup (1 stick) butter

2   grouse breasts

Salt and freshly ground black pepper

1½ cups cold water

1   small carrot, cut into ¼-inch-thick slices

1   small Vidalia onion, cut into ¼-inch-thick slices

1   celery rib, cut into ¼-inch-thick slices

2   fresh parsley sprigs

½   bay leaf

¼   cup all-purpose flour

¾   cup canned diced tomatoes

1   teaspoon fresh lemon juice

1   teaspoon minced fresh parsley

½   cup sautéed mushrooms

1. Melt ¼ cup butter in a 10-inch cast iron skillet over medium heat. Add breasts; brown both sides. Season with salt and pepper to taste. Pour the water over the top. Add the carrot and next 4 ingredients. Cover and simmer over low heat until tender, 20 minutes.

2. Remove the breasts from the pan, strain the stock, and set aside. Rinse and dry the skillet.

3. Melt the remaining ¼ cup butter in pan over low heat; stir in flour, whisking until golden brown. Add reserved stock and tomatoes gradually to the roux, stirring constantly. Add the lemon juice, parsley, and mushrooms; season with salt and pepper to taste. Remove and discard bay leaf. Reheat the grouse in the sauce and serve.

SEARED PEPPER STEAK WITH BOURBON-SHALLOT SAUCE

serves 4

Contributed by Chris Schlesinger, chef/owner of the East Coast Grill in Cambridge, Massachusetts, this recipe was perfected by his father, who cooked it for special occasions. A cast iron skillet is the key to providing a flavor-packed crust, but beware: This technique also creates a lot of smoke. "My dad always claimed the smoke contributed to the atmosphere," recalls Chris. "Both the aroma and the flavor will always be embedded in my culinary memory."

2   tablespoons kosher salt, plus more to taste

¼   cup cracked black peppercorns

4   (10-ounce) beef top loin steaks, about 1 inch thick

2   tablespoons olive oil

3   tablespoons chopped shallots

½   cup bourbon

½   cup beef stock

¼   cup heavy cream

1   tablespoon butter

2   tablespoons chopped fresh parsley

1. Rub the salt and cracked peppercorns on both sides of the steaks.

2. Heat the oil in a large cast iron skillet over medium-high heat until hot. Cook the steaks 3 to 4 minutes per side for medium rare or to desired degree of doneness. Transfer the steaks to a plate and loosely cover with foil.

3. Add the shallots to the skillet and sauté 30 seconds.

4. Remove the skillet from the heat and turn off the burner. Add the

bourbon (there will be a lot of steam all at once). Carefully light the liquid in the skillet with a long match. Allow the flames to burn off on their own.

5. Return the skillet to the heat. Add the stock, bring it to a simmer, and cook until the liquid is reduced by half, about 3 minutes. Stir in the cream and simmer 3 minutes.

6. Remove the pan from the heat and stir in the butter until totally incorporated into the sauce. Stir in the parsley. Taste and add additional salt to taste, if desired.

7. Place a steak on each of 4 plates, top with the sauce, and serve.

Cast Iron Grilled Steaks with Blue Cheese Butter

CAST IRON GRILLED STEAKS WITH BLUE CHEESE BUTTER

serves 2

For cooking instructor and food writer Jane Gaither, known in Tennessee as "Gourmet Gadget Gal," the secret to grilling restaurant-quality steaks at home means pulling out her Lodge grill pan, quickly searing the steaks on the stove, and finishing them in the oven. This recipe goes from stove-top to table in 10 minutes.

Blue Cheese Butter:

$^1/_2$ cup (1 stick) unsalted butter, softened

1 (4-ounce) package crumbled blue cheese

1 teaspoon Worcestershire sauce

Pinch of salt

A few grinds of black pepper

Steaks:

2 (1-inch-thick) beef strip steaks

1 teaspoon vegetable oil

Salt and freshly ground black pepper

1. Cream the butter in a small bowl, then add the blue cheese, Worcestershire, salt, and pepper and beat until smooth. Using a 12-inch piece of plastic wrap, spoon out the butter mixture and roll it up like a log, twisting the ends. Freeze the butter until firm or for up to 1 month.

2. Preheat the oven to 350°.

3. Bring the steaks to room temperature. Heat a Lodge Grill Pan over high heat until smoking hot. Carefully brush the pan with the oil.

4. Season the steaks on both sides with salt and pepper to taste. Carefully place the steaks on the hot grill pan and grill 2 minutes per

side.

5. Transfer the grill pan to the oven and bake for 2 minutes.

6. Remove the pan from the oven and let the steaks stand 5 minutes. Serve with a pat of Blue Cheese Butter on each steak.

Pan-fried Fajita Steaks

PAN-FRIED FAJITA STEAKS

serves 4

Fajitas are a restaurant favorite, but John Meyer of Main Dish Media has started making them at home—and they've become a regular request when friends come over. He cooks the steaks and vegetables in cast iron skillets, and serves the fajitas straight out of the pans. "Unlike most fajita recipes, I use whole steaks, as well as big cuts of vegetables. If I wanted small slices and bites, I'd be doing stir-fry!" John explains. When left whole, the steaks develop a flavorful sear, while the whole vegetables retain their individual taste and texture.

2   tablespoons chili powder

1   tablespoon dried oregano

1   tablespoon ground cumin

2   teaspoons kosher salt, plus more to taste

2   teaspoons freshly ground black pepper, plus more to taste

4   (10-to 12-ounce) beef strip steaks

3   tablespoons vegetable oil

8   fajita-style flour tortillas

2   yellow bell peppers, cut in half and seeded

8   plum tomatoes, cut in half

12 green onions, trimmed

2   limes, cut in half

1. Preheat the oven to 350°. Preheat 2 large cast iron skillets over medium-high heat.

2. Combine the chili powder, oregano, cumin, salt, and pepper in a small bowl; rub the mixture evenly over the steaks.

3. Pour 1 tablespoon oil into each of the hot skillets. Add 2 steaks to each pan and sear, turning every minute, until the steaks reach

desired degree of doneness (10 to 12 minutes or an internal temperature of 120° for medium rare). Transfer the steaks to a platter, cover loosely with foil, and let stand.

4. Wrap the tortillas in foil and warm in the oven as the vegetables cook.

5. Increase the heat under the skillets to high. Add some of the remaining 1 tablespoon oil to each pan, if necessary. Divide the bell peppers, tomatoes, green onions, and lime halves into 2 equal piles; add to the hot pans. Cook, tossing the vegetables and limes a few times, until slightly charred, 3 to 4 minutes. Transfer the mixture to the platter with the steaks.

6. To serve, heat both skillets over high heat; return the steaks and fajita vegetables to the pans and squeeze the charred lime halves over the top. Serve with the warm tortillas. Each diner gets their own steak and can help themselves to the vegetables in the pans.

SUKIYAKI

serves 4 to 6

Growing up in Sacramento, Michael McLaughlin especially looked forward to sukiyaki dinners out with his family. Whether served ready to eat, with the pot's contents ladled into the diners' waiting bowls, or the raw ingredients assembled on platters for diners to cook at the table using the sizzling broth from a Japanese hot-pot, sukiyaki is a festive meal. Michael invites you to try his favorite recipe adapted for the home cook.

$1\frac{1}{2}$ cups dashi ($\frac{1}{4}$ teaspoon instant bonito-flavored soup stock powder added to 1 cup lukewarm water), or vegetable or beef stock, or water

$\frac{1}{2}$ cup soy sauce

$\frac{1}{2}$ cup mirin (sweet rice wine)

2   to 4 tablespoons brown sugar

$\frac{1}{4}$ cup sake (optional)

1   (7-ounce) block enoki mushrooms

5   baby bok choy or ½ head napa (Chinese) cabbage

2   teaspoons canola oil

1   (14-ounce) package firm tofu, drained and cut into ½-inch cubes

1   pound high-quality, well-marbled boneless sirloin or rib-eye steak, cut into ¼-inch-thick slices

1   bunch leafy greens (watercress, spinach, edible chrysanthemum leaves, Swiss chard, etc.), trimmed of heavy stems and cut into bite-size pieces

8   small to medium shiitake mushrooms, stemmed

2   green onions, trimmed and cut into 1-inch pieces

1   (8-ounce) package shirataki noodles

1. In a medium bowl, stir together the dashi, soy sauce, mirin, brown sugar to taste, and, if desired, sake, until the brown sugar dissolves.

2. Cut off and discard the connective bottom from the block of enoki mushrooms, pulling them apart under cool running water. Soak for about 2 minutes; drain and set aside. Trim the bottoms from the bok choy and slice across into ½-inch-wide strips.

3. Heat a cast iron Dutch oven over medium heat until hot. Heat the oil, and then sear the tofu until browned on all sides, about 8 minutes. Remove the tofu from the Dutch oven.

4. Add the steak to the Dutch oven and stir-fry until about 80% of the desired degree of doneness, about 3 minutes. Remove from the pot.

5. Add the bok choy and greens and stir-fry just until wilted, 1 to 2 minutes. Remove from the pot.

6. Add the enoki and shiitake mushrooms and green onions and stir-fry to soften, 1 to 2 minutes.

7. Return the greens, bok choy, and tofu to the Dutch oven. Add the shirataki noodles. Stir the dashi mixture; pour over mixture in Dutch oven and bring to a simmer. Add the steak and stir. Bring the pot to the table and let diners serve themselves.

{ Asian flavor }

From an Asian market you will need shirataki noodles, also known as yam noodles. They come in a package, ready to use, and look similar to moistened glass noodles. The recipe also calls for the bonito-flavored soup stock known as dashi, and mirin, a sweetened cooking rice wine.

BOURBON BARREL PEPPER POT ROAST

serves 4

This recipe is from Francine Maroukian, an award-winning food writer and contributing editor to *Garden & Gun, Travel + Leisure*, and *Esquire* magazines.

1   (3$\frac{1}{2}$-pound) chuck roast

Coarse salt

Bourbon smoked pepper

2   tablespoons canola oil

2   cups beef stock

2   tablespoons tomato paste

4   cups ($\frac{1}{2}$-inch-thick) diagonally sliced carrots

2   tablespoons sorghum syrup

Hot seasoned rice

1. Preheat the oven to 325°.

2. Pat the roast dry with paper towels and season it liberally with salt and smoked pepper to taste.

3. Heat the oil in a large cast iron Dutch oven over high heat until hot but not smoking. (The oil will appear to be moving in waves across the surface of the pot and shimmer slightly.) Sear the roast in the hot oil, rotating it with tongs to brown all sides. Remove the roast from the

pan.

4. Combine the stock and tomato paste in a bowl and stir until well blended; slowly add the stock mixture to the pan, scraping the pan bottom to loosen browned bits.

5. Reduce the heat to low, return the roast to the pan, and bring the liquid to a low boil. Cover the pan, transfer it to the oven, and bake until the roast is fork-tender, about $2\frac{3}{4}$ hours.

6. Transfer the roast to a cutting board. Place the Dutch oven on the stove-top; add the carrots and cook at a low simmer until tender, about 10 minutes. Whisk in the sorghum and bring to a simmer to thicken, no longer than 3 minutes; immediately remove from the heat.

7. Slice the meat thickly and serve in shallow bowls with seasoned rice. Spoon the sauce and carrots over the top and sprinkle on a bit more smoked pepper.

{ sorghum syrup }

Sorghum is a sweet syrup with a hint of exotic spice; it can be purchased (as can the bourbon smoked pepper) at _bourbonbarrelfoods.com_.

Rolled Flank Steak

ROLLED FLANK STEAK

serves 4 to 6

International Dutch Oven Society members Nicole and Taylor Baugh contributed this beautiful and tasty dish, perfect to present to guests.

1	(2-pound) flank steak
$1/2$	cup olive oil
$1/4$	cup soy sauce
2	teaspoons steak seasoning and more to taste
2	tablespoons chopped garlic
$1/2$	pound thinly sliced provolone cheese
4	thick bacon slices
$1/2$	cup baby spinach
$1/2$	cup sliced cremini mushrooms
$1/2$	red bell pepper, seeded and cut into strips
$1/2$	cup chopped onion

1. Place the flank steak on a cutting board with a short end facing you. Starting from one of the long sides, cut through the meat horizontally to within $1/2$ inch of the opposite edge.

2. Combine the oil, soy sauce, and steak seasoning in a 1-gallon zip-top plastic freezer bag. Add the steak, zip the bag shut, and squeeze to coat the steak. Marinate in the refrigerator 4 hours or overnight.

3. Preheat the oven to 350°. Grease a large cast iron Dutch oven.

4. Lay out the flank steak flat in front of you with the grain of the meat running from left to right. Spread the garlic evenly over the meat and sprinkle with steak seasoning to taste. Layer the provolone over the steak, leaving a 1-inch border on all sides. Arrange the bacon, spinach, mushrooms, bell pepper, and onion over the cheese in stripes running in the same direction as the grain of the meat. Roll the flank steak up and away from you so that when the roll is cut into the pinwheel shape, each of the filling ingredients can be seen; roll firmly, but be careful not to squeeze the fillings out the ends. Once rolled, tie with kitchen string, securing at 2-inch intervals.

5. Place the stuffed steak into the prepared Dutch oven and bake until a meat thermometer inserted in the center of the stuffed steak registers 145°, about 1 hour. Remove the stuffed steak from the Dutch oven and let stand 5 to 10 minutes before cutting into 1-inch-thick slices. Remove the string before serving.

Some cooks mistakenly shy away from cast iron when a recipe contains an acid like tomatoes or vinegar. The simple fact is that if your cast iron is well seasoned, the iron is impervious to whatever you decide to put into your pan. And for Nach Waxman, owner of Kitchen Arts & Letters bookstore in New York City, cast iron is his pan of choice when cooking up (or rather cooking down) this tomato reduction.

A SUMMER TOMATO REDUCTION

When I'm lucky and am faced with a good tomato season and a magnificent end-of-summer surplus of big, squishy tomatoes going soft faster than one could ever use them; the solution, of course, is to make sauce. But sauce, whether you can it or freeze it, requires a fair amount of prep work and, after you've made it, you've got quarts and quarts to be stored—no casual consideration in most modern homes.

So, with the help of cast iron, I've adopted a method of getting the bulk down, freezing it, and giving our household a terrific pantry resource for those difficult, tomato-deprived winter months. When you thaw this highly flavored base, you can add garlic, sausage, or whatever you like, simmer it together with good canned tomatoes, and bring a range of surprisingly fresh and interesting sauces to your winter table.

TOMATO REDUCTION RECIPE

makes 8 (4-ounce) containers

This recipe is for reducing 2 quarts (8 cups) of tomatoes at a time, which is a good, efficient cooking unit.

6   to 9 ripe tomatoes, depending on their size

2   to 3 tablespoons olive oil, plus 1 teaspoon, as needed

$1/_2$ cup finely chopped white bottom portion of celery ribs

$1/_2$ cup torn celery leaves

Up to 2 rounded tablespoons Part Pesto or about 20 large fresh basil leaves, torn into small pieces, to your taste

1   to 2 tablespoons water, as needed

Salt and freshly ground black pepper

1. Cut the stems and any bad spots out of the tomatoes. Cut the tomatoes into $3/_8$-inch-thick slices, and then cut each slice into $3/_8$-inch cubes. Do this over a plate to catch any juices.

2. Heat 2 to 3 tablespoons oil in a 10-or 12-inch cast iron skillet over medium heat. Reduce the heat slightly; add the chopped celery and leaves and cook until softened and the leaves start to darken (don't let them brown), stirring occasionally. Add the cubed tomatoes along with any spilled juices and pulp and start them bubbling slowly but steadily; reduce them for 30 minutes.

3. Add the Part Pesto and cook 5 minutes. Reduce the heat to the lowest setting and cook very slowly for at least 2 hours, stirring every half hour or so, making certain that there is no sticking. If there is, add the water and remaining 1 teaspoon oil, as needed, and scrape up any stuck portions. You will notice that the water will gradually evaporate until what remains is extremely thick but still damp with a small amount of oil. It will be about the density of a relish, and the tomatoes will appear to be a softer, much less intense version of the sun-dried product.

4. Season the reduction with salt and pepper to taste. Let cool completely; divide among airtight containers and freeze.

PART PESTO

Part Pesto is a pesto prepared in season, when fresh basil is abundant, and then frozen. It is made by blending basil leaves, olive oil, salt, pine nuts, and a little water, omitting the garlic and cheese, which do not survive the freezing very well. Because of its oil and salt content, it freezes nicely into an intense, pungent slurry, which has the texture of ice cream and can be conveniently spooned out as needed. For 2 cups *fresh basil leaves*, I add *½ cup olive oil, ¼ cup pine nuts, and ¼ cup water*. This preparation, intended for freezing, is a modified version of a suggestion by Paula Wolfert in her book *Mediterranean Cooking*.

STEAK, KIDNEY, AND MUSHROOM PIE

serves 4

Chef/owner Patrick Reilly, of the Majestic Grille in Memphis, is a huge fan of beef kidney, but he understands that not everyone shares his enthusiasm. If that's the case, he advises you to simply use more beef.

$\frac{1}{2}$ pound beef kidney (buy it from your local butcher)

$\frac{1}{4}$ cup all-purpose flour

Kosher salt and freshly ground black pepper

2 tablespoons vegetable oil

1 pound beef stew meat, cut into 1-inch pieces (Patrick loves the beef from Neola Farms in Tipton County, Tennessee, but, failing that, advises that you buy your meat from a good local butcher and cube it yourself; avoid pre-packaged stew meat)

4 thick bacon slices, cut into 1-inch pieces

1 medium onion, cut into $\frac{1}{4}$-inch cubes

1 celery rib, diced

2 garlic cloves, chopped

4 ounces button mushrooms, quartered

$\frac{1}{2}$ of a (12-ounce) bottle beer (use a good brown ale such as Bass or Guinness Stout)

$\frac{1}{2}$ cup red wine

1 cup beef stock

2 bay leaves

1 fresh thyme sprig

1 (17.3-ounce) package frozen puff pastry sheets, thawed

1 egg yolk, beaten with 2 teaspoons water and a pinch of salt

1. Cut the kidney in half and remove any tubes and skin. Cut into 1-inch pieces and soak in ice water for about 1 hour. Drain and pat dry.

2. Place the flour in a shallow bowl and season generously with salt and pepper to taste.

3. Heat the oil in a 12-inch cast iron skillet over medium-high heat until hazy but not smoking.

4. Dredge the beef and kidney pieces in the flour, shaking off any excess. Brown the beef and kidney in the hot oil on all sides in 2 batches. Remove from the pan and keep warm.

5. Reduce the heat to medium, add the bacon, and cook for a few minutes. Add the onion and celery and cook until lightly browned, stirring a few times. Add the garlic and mushrooms and cook, stirring often, for a few minutes. Add the beer and wine and reduce by three-fourths. Add the stock, bay leaves, thyme, and browned meat. Cover, reduce the heat to low, and simmer until the beef and kidney pieces are tender, about 1 hour.

6. Remove the bay leaves and thyme. Allow the filling to cool in the pan to room temperature; cover with plastic wrap and refrigerate overnight.

7. Preheat the oven to 350°.

8. Roll the pastry into a 13-inch circle on a lightly floured surface with a floured rolling pin. Cover the chilled pan with the pastry; it should overhang the edge of the pan slightly, about $1/4$ inch. Brush the pastry with the egg wash. Bake until the pastry is golden brown and the filling is heated through, 20 to 30 minutes. Serve immediately or the crust will start to get soggy.

{ perfect crust }

Traditionally in the making of steak and kidney pie, a pie pan is lined with pastry, the cooked meat is poured in, and then it is covered with the top pastry. Baked that way, Patrick Reilly always found the pastry to be soggy. His solution is to cook the filling in a cast iron skillet and chill it overnight. The next day, cover it with puff pastry right in the pan. The result—piping hot beef and a crispy, crumbly crust.

GRILLADES

serves 6

According to Chef John D. Folse, founder and namesake of the John Folse Culinary Institute at Nicholls State University in Thibodaux, Louisiana, it is believed this dish originated when South Louisiana butchers preparing the annual *boucherie* took thin pieces of fresh pork and pan-fried them with sliced onions. The cooking probably took place in black iron pots hung over the *boucherie* fires. The grillades were eaten over grits or rice throughout the day. Today, grillades and grits are a tradition on many Sunday brunch menus. To present grillades as an entrée, serve it over rice. Most recipes for grillades call for veal round pounded lightly and smothered in natural juices. This recipe is from Chef Folse's book *The Encyclopedia of Cajun & Creole Cuisine.*

2   medium veal or beef round steaks (1 to $1\frac{1}{2}$ pounds total)

Salt

Cracked black peppercorns

1   cup all-purpose flour

$\frac{1}{4}$ cup vegetable shortening or bacon drippings

1   cup minced onion

1   cup minced celery

$\frac{1}{2}$ cup minced bell pepper

1   cup diced tomatoes

1   cup thinly sliced green onions

$\frac{1}{4}$ cup minced garlic

3   cups beef stock

1   cup sliced mushrooms

¼   cup chopped fresh parsley

1. Cut the round steaks into 3-inch squares. Season with salt and cracked peppercorns to taste. Dust the pieces generously with the flour.

2. Melt the shortening in a large cast iron Dutch oven over medium-high heat. Brown the meat (in batches, if necessary) on all sides. Add the onion, celery, bell pepper, tomatoes, green onions, and garlic; cook, stirring, until the vegetables are wilted, 3 to 5 minutes. Pour in the stock and bring to a low boil; reduce the heat to a simmer. Cover the pan and cook the grillades slowly, stirring occasionally to prevent scorching, until the meat is tender, about 45 minutes.

3. Stir in the mushrooms and parsley. Adjust the seasonings, if necessary. Cook 10 minutes, and serve over grits or rice.

Shepherd's Pie

SHEPHERD'S PIE

serves 8

This recipe is from Paul Kelly, a network instructor for Pitney Bowes. An excellent cook and lifelong devotee of Lodge cast iron, Paul regularly prepares dishes for family and friends in his Senoia, Georgia, home. Shepherd's pie is usually made using ground beef, but preparing it with tender pot roast makes it irresistible.

Filling:

4 tablespoons extra-virgin olive oil

2 pounds chuck roast or other beef stew meat with the fat trimmed, cut into 1-inch cubes

1 large Vidalia onion, chopped

4 garlic cloves, minced

2 teaspoons salt, plus more to taste

1 teaspoon freshly ground black pepper

1 teaspoon red pepper flakes (optional)

1 cup beef broth

1 teaspoon dried oregano

1 teaspoon dried thyme

1 tablespoon chopped fresh flat-leaf parsley

4 large carrots, cut into 1-inch pieces, or $1^{1}/_{2}$ cups baby carrots

$1^{1}/_{2}$ cups frozen green peas

1 cup chopped celery

2 tablespoons all-purpose flour

1 cup water

Mashed Potato Crust:

2 pounds baking potatoes, peeled and cut into 1-inch cubes

4 quarts water

1   tablespoon salt
3   tablespoons salted butter
1/2   cup milk
1/2   cup half-and-half
1   teaspoon freshly ground black pepper

1. Make the filling: Preheat the oven to 325°. Heat 2 tablespoons oil in a 5-quart cast iron Dutch oven over medium-high heat. Add the beef, half the onion, half the garlic, the salt, black pepper, and, if desired, red pepper to the pan and cook until the beef is browned on all sides, about 5 minutes. Add the broth, oregano, thyme, and parsley. Cover the pan and transfer to the oven; bake until the meat is fork-tender, about 2 hours.

2. Remove the meat and broth and wipe the pan clean. Place the remaining 2 tablespoons oil in the pan and heat over medium-high heat. Add the remaining onion and garlic and cook, stirring often, 2 minutes. Add the carrots, peas, and celery and cook, stirring often, 2 minutes.

3. Return the meat to the pan, stir, and add enough of the broth to cover. Season with salt to taste. Cook over medium heat, stirring frequently, 5 minutes.

4. Place the flour in a cup and slowly add the water, whisking until smooth; if any lumps form, strain the flour mixture through a sieve. Add the flour mixture to the pan and stir well to blend.

5. Increase the oven temperature to 350°.

6. Make the mashed potato crust: Place the potatoes in a stockpot; add the water and salt and bring to a boil. Cook until potatoes are tender, about 10 minutes. Drain thoroughly. While the potatoes are still hot, stir in the butter until it melts. Add the milk, half-and-half, and pepper; mash until smooth.

7. Spoon the mashed potatoes over the filling in the Dutch oven. Bake on the center rack, uncovered, 30 minutes.

8. Turn on the broiler and broil until the potatoes are browned, about

5 minutes. Check often to prevent burning.

ALL-AMERICAN SHORT RIBS

serves 4

Tough and bony short ribs are delicious when braised until fall-off-the-bone tender. In this Southern-style version, from Joanna Pruess' *Cast-Iron Cookbook: Delicious and Simple Comfort Food*, the cooking liquid includes bourbon and molasses. (Joanna likes the robust, slightly less sweet taste of dark molasses, but you can also use the light variety.)

4   pounds bone-in beef short ribs, trimmed and blotted dry
Salt and freshly ground black pepper
Grapeseed or canola oil
2   medium carrots, diced
1   medium yellow onion, diced
1   large celery rib, diced
1   tablespoon minced garlic
$^1/_2$ cup bourbon
$1^1/_2$ cups beef stock
1   (14$^1/_2$-ounce) can diced tomatoes, undrained
$^1/_2$ cup molasses
3   large fresh thyme sprigs or 1 tablespoon dried thyme
2   bay leaves
2   tablespoons chopped fresh flat-leaf parsley

1. Preheat the oven to 350°.

2. Season the short ribs on both sides with salt and pepper to taste. Heat a large cast iron Dutch oven over high heat until hot, about 3 minutes. Pour in about 1 tablespoon oil and add as many ribs as can fit comfortably in the bottom of the pan without crowding (cook in

batches, if necessary); sear them on all sides. Remove the browned ribs to a large bowl. Add oil as needed to the pan and repeat until all the ribs are cooked.

3. Drain all but 1 tablespoon of the drippings from the pan. Stir in the carrots, onion, and celery; cook over medium-high heat, stirring often, until lightly browned, about 5 minutes. Stir in the garlic and cook 30 seconds; pour in the bourbon and boil over high heat until almost evaporated, about $1^1/_2$ minutes. Add the stock, tomatoes and their juice, molasses, thyme, and bay leaves; return the ribs to the pan and bring to a boil. Cover the pan and transfer it to the oven to bake until the meat is fork-tender, $1^1/_2$ to 2 hours.

4. Remove from the oven. Using tongs, transfer the short ribs to a bowl. Pour the liquid through a strainer to catch vegetables, and then pour the broth into a fat separator; discard the fat and return the liquid to the pan. (If you don't have a fat separator, cover the pan and refrigerate it overnight or until the fat congeals; scrape off the fat, return the sauce to the pan, and heat.) Return the meat and strained vegetables to the liquid in the pan; cover, heat, and set aside. If the sauce is too thin, gently boil to reduce and slightly thicken it, spooning it over the ribs and turning them occasionally. Add additional salt and pepper to taste, if desired. Discard the bay leaves and thyme stems; sprinkle with the parsley and serve.

{ short ribs }

Short ribs are generally sold in 1-and 2-inch lengths. The shorter ones are easier to work with, but with either size, you should figure about a pound of uncooked ribs per person. You can make these several days ahead, refrigerate them, and then slowly reheat them before serving. Serve over grits or mashed potatoes.

SEARED PORK CHOPS WITH CARAMELIZED APPLES AND ONIONS

serves 2

In this recipe, Bri Malaspino, creative manager of Lodge Manufacturing, enhances New England-style pork chops with the crispy sear and sweet caramelized flavors only cast iron can provide. This recipe is traditionally made by layering the items in a roasting dish and baking it, which yields a more stewed flavor. By sautéing and searing the ingredients, you get a greater contrast in flavors and texture.

3 tablespoons butter

1 Granny Smith apple, cored and cut into $\frac{1}{2}$- to 1-inch-thick slices

1 sweet onion, cut into $\frac{1}{2}$-inch-thick rings

3 to 5 fresh sage leaves, chopped

2 large (1-inch-thick) bone-in pork chops

Salt and freshly ground black pepper

1. Melt 2 tablespoons butter in a 12-inch cast iron skillet over medium heat. Add the apple slices, onion rings, and sage; cook, turning the mixture occasionally, until the apple and onion are caramelized. Remove the mixture from the pan and keep warm.

2. Increase the heat to medium-high. Add the remaining 1 tablespoon butter to the pan.

3. Season the pork chops with salt and pepper to taste. Add the pork chops to the pan and sear 6 to 8 minutes per side for medium doneness or 10 to 14 minutes per side for well done. For the best results, cover the pan for the last 10 minutes of cooking time to trap as much moisture as possible.

4. Serve the chops with the sautéed apple and onion.

Pan Pork with Rapid Ratatouille

PAN PORK WITH RAPID RATATOUILLE

serves 4

This recipe is from Francine Maroukian, an award-winning food writer and contributing editor to *Garden & Gun, Travel + Leisure*, and *Esquire* magazines. "Be sure to make this with small, firm squash," she advises. "Larger squash hold so much water that you'll get steamed rather than browned vegetables."

1   ($2^1/_2$-pound) boneless pork loin

Salt and freshly ground black pepper

2   tablespoons canola oil

2   tablespoons unsalted butter

1   shallot, minced

2   garlic cloves, minced

4   cups diced mixed pattypan squash and zucchini

1   cup diced tomatoes

Big pinch of torn fresh herbs (like basil, parsley, or thyme)

1. Preheat the oven to 375°.

2. Season the pork loin with salt and pepper to taste.

3. Heat a cast iron skillet over medium heat until hot. Add the oil and sear the pork loin on all sides. Transfer the skillet to the oven and roast until a meat thermometer inserted into the thickest portion registers 155° and the pork is cooked through but still juicy, about 25 minutes. Transfer the pork to a cutting board to stand.

4. Return the skillet to medium heat. Add the butter and let it melt, stirring frequently to scrape up any browned bits. When the butter is foaming slightly, add the shallot and garlic, stirring quickly to soften. As soon as they release their fragrances (about $1^1/_2$ minutes), add the squash mix and stir to coat with the flavored butter. Cook, stirring occasionally, until golden brown, about 6 minutes. Add the tomatoes

and herbs; stir only once or twice to soften the tomatoes and release the aroma of the herbs.

5. Slice the pork loin and place on 4 plates. Spoon the ratatouille onto the pork slices, adding salt and pepper to taste, if desired.

LOMO DE PUERCO ASADO *(Roasted Pork Loin)*

serves 6 to 8

This recipe from *Sunset* food editor Margo True is a reimagining of a dish her father made frequently when their family lived for several years in Mexico—first in Guadalajara and later in Tijuana. It's an easy main course, and leftovers make good pork sandwiches—especially layered on a crusty Mexican *bolillo* or other white roll, with avocado, cilantro, tomato, and sweet onion.

1   cup olive oil

$1\frac{1}{2}$ tablespoons fresh lime juice

$1\frac{1}{2}$ teaspoons dried Mexican oregano or 1 tablespoon chopped fresh oregano

1   teaspoon dried crushed chile de arbol or red pepper flakes

1   teaspoon ground cumin

1   teaspoon salt

$\frac{1}{2}$ teaspoon freshly ground black pepper

3   garlic cloves, crushed

1   (3-pound) boneless pork loin roast

2   tablespoons vegetable oil

1. Whisk together the first 8 ingredients in a small bowl. Place the pork in a baking dish just big enough to hold it, pour the marinade over the top, and turn to coat. Marinate, covered, in the refrigerator at least 12 hours (preferably 24 hours), turning once or twice.

2. Let the pork stand 1 hour or until it reaches room temperature.

3. Preheat the oven to 350°.

4. Heat the vegetable oil in a large cast iron skillet over medium-high heat. Remove the pork from the marinade and discard the marinade.

Pat the pork dry with paper towels; add the pork to the pan and brown well on all sides, about 10 minutes.

5. Transfer the skillet to the oven and roast until a meat thermometer inserted in the thickest portion registers 140° (the temperature will rise after the meat comes out of the oven), 45 to 60 minutes. Let the roast stand, covered loosely with foil, 15 minutes before slicing.

{ note }

There was a time when folks worried about trichinosis in fresh pork and therefore overcooked it to eliminate these fears. Trichinosis has been all but eliminated from commercial pork. But even when an infestation is present, spores are killed when the meat reaches an internal temperature of 137°, well below the doneness recommended to produce juicy pork. Cook to 150° to 155°. Perfect pork will have a faint pink blush. Let it stand for 10 to 15 minutes after cooking to reabsorb juices and allow the meat to finish cooking (raising the internal termperature by 5° to 10°; the USDA recommends cooking pork to 160°).

CARNITAS *(Mexican Pulled Pork Tacos)*

serves 8 to 14, depending on the appetites!

Cooler weather is the perfect time for braised dishes, which fill the house with savory and comforting smells. This recipe from Al Hernandez, food and wine editor of *The Vine Times*, provides an easy and inexpensive option for a festive group.

2   tablespoons granulated garlic

2   tablespoons paprika

1   tablespoon kosher salt, plus more to taste

1   teaspoon freshly ground black pepper, plus more to taste

$1/2$ teaspoon cayenne pepper

1   (4-to 6-pound) bone-in pork shoulder (also known as Boston butt or picnic roast)

2   tablespoons vegetable oil

1   medium yellow onion, chopped

3   cups chicken stock

12   to 24 flour or corn tortillas, warmed

Toppings: chopped onion, chopped cilantro, shredded cheese, chopped tomato, guacamole, and/or salsa

1. Preheat the oven to 225°.

2. Combine the granulated garlic, paprika, salt, black pepper, and cayenne in a small bowl. Rub the spice mixture over the pork shoulder.

3. Heat a large cast iron Dutch oven over medium heat. Add the oil and onion and cook, stirring often, until softened. Place the pork shoulder in the pan and pour in the stock. Cover and slow roast for 8 hours, turning the pork after 4 hours.

4. Transfer the pork to a cutting board or platter and shred with two

forks. Season the pork and the cooking liquid (save this liquid and use it as a base for soup) with additional salt and pepper, if desired.

5. Serve the pork with the tortillas topped with your favorite taco toppings.

crazy for cast iron

I don't think I knew there was any type of skillet other than cast iron until I was 9 or 10 years old. Things were either cooked in cast iron or on the grill during the summer. I assumed everyone used cast iron. This, of course, was reinforced by my favorite Saturday morning cartoons—someone was bound to get hit with a frying pan at some point!

It wasn't until years later that I realized why it seemed to be the only type of skillet to me as a child. The versatility of cast iron crosses all boundaries, from searing to sautéing, baking to braising—one pan can do it all. As an added bonus, if properly taken care of, it will last for generations. Just ask Grandma or your favorite Saturday morning cartoon character!   —Al Hernandez

One of the most efficient and satisfying ways of making a dressing for pasta that can be prepared in as little time as it takes to cook up and drain the pasta involves using a good heavy cast iron pan—a 10-or 12-inch, depending on the amount of pasta you are making. Typically it involves heating olive oil over a relatively high flame and adding any of a number of ingredients to the oil and sizzling them a bit —cut-up anchovies or sardines, garlic, coarse black pepper, red pepper flakes, capers, chopped parsley, broccoli rabe, a handful of quartered cherry tomatoes, etc. Don't add too many different things, perhaps two or three, because this is meant to be a simple preparation. And, of course, the order and the timing depend on the ingredients used. For example, garlic normally goes in toward the very end so that it doesn't brown and begin to turn bitter.

I often prepare one of these for myself and my wife, Maron, to serve with a thin spaghetti. When the pasta is finished, but definitely al dente, I drain it and promptly dump it, still damp, into the hot flavored oil and the infused ingredients, tossing it for a minute or two over a good medium hot flame. I use tongs to keep it moving and well mixed. Then, I continue cooking it in the pan for about 5 minutes more, turning it only two or three times. In this way, some of the pasta surfaces begin to crisp and even brown a bit.

I serve it straight out of the pan at the table. It looks good, tastes zesty, and every mouthful contains a little bit of crunch. If you like, finish it off with a grating of cheese.   —Nach Waxman

BRAISED PORK SHOULDER WITH STAR ANISE

serves 8 to 10

This recipe is a favorite of mother and daughter cookbook authors Sharon Kramis and Julie Kramis Hearne, who serve it over polenta, mashed potatoes, risotto, or noodles. They like to use any leftover pork to make sandwiches with coleslaw and mango salsa the next day.

1   (3-to 4-pound) bone-in pork shoulder
1   teaspoon salt, plus more to taste
$\frac{1}{2}$ teaspoon freshly ground black pepper, plus more to taste
2   tablespoons olive oil
1   medium yellow onion, cut in half and medium diced
3   garlic cloves, slivered
1   cup beef broth
1   ($14\frac{1}{2}$-ounce) can fire-roasted diced tomatoes, undrained (such as Muir Glen)
$\frac{1}{2}$ cup full-bodied red wine
2   tablespoons brown sugar
1   cinnamon stick
3   star anise
1   bay leaf

1. Preheat the oven to 325°.

2. Score the fat side of the pork shoulder in a crisscross pattern. Pat dry and season all over with the salt and pepper.

3. Heat the oil in a 5-quart cast iron Dutch oven over medium to medium-high heat. Cook the pork, turning it using tongs or a long

fork, until browned on all sides, 8 to 10 minutes. Transfer the pork to a large plate and set aside.

4. Add the onion to the pan drippings and cook over medium heat, stirring occasionally, 5 minutes. Add the garlic and cook, stirring often, 3 minutes. Add the broth, tomatoes (with their juice), and wine. Bring to a low boil and stir in the brown sugar; add the cinnamon stick, star anise, and bay leaf. Return the pork to the pan and cover with a tight-fitting lid. Transfer to the center rack of the oven and braise until the pork is fork-tender, $2\frac{1}{2}$ to 3 hours.

5. Transfer the pork to a serving platter with tongs or a long fork. Bring the juices in the pan to a boil and cook until reduced and slightly thickened, about 3 minutes. Season with more salt and pepper, to taste, if desired. Discard the cinnamon stick, star anise, and bay leaf. Slice the pork and drizzle the sauce over the top.

INDOOR PULLED PORK WITH NORTH CAROLINA VINEGAR SAUCE

serves 8

Grilling expert and cookbook author Elizabeth Karmel dedicates this recipe to Lodge public relations and advertising manager, Mark Kelly. He loves Elizabeth's slow-smoked North Carolina pulled pork so much that he convinced her to try adapting it to a Dutch oven. "At first, I thought it would be blasphemy, but once I tried it, I had to agree that it was a quick and easy version that is great for winter, tailgates, and anyone who doesn't have outdoor space," says Elizabeth. If you cook it on top of the stove the entire time, you will need two to three times the liquid as you do for the oven method. This recipe is adapted from one in Elizabeth's cookbook *Taming the Flame: Secrets for Hot-and-Quick and Low-and-Slow BBQ.*

1   (4-to 7-pound) bone-in pork shoulder or Boston butt, trimmed
Olive oil
Kosher salt and freshly ground black pepper
<u>North Carolina Vinegar Sauce</u>
2   cups water
1   package hamburger buns (no sesame seeds)
<u>North Carolina Coleslaw</u>

1. Pat the pork dry with paper towels and then brush with a thin coating of oil. Season with salt and pepper to taste.

2. Heat about 2 tablespoons oil in a 9-quart cast iron Dutch oven over medium-high heat until hot. Gently lower the pork into the pan and sear 3 to 4 minutes on all sides; you want the pork to be golden brown. While the pork is searing, make the North Carolina Vinegar Sauce.

3. Once the pork is seared, arrange it in the pan so that the fat side is facing up. Pour the water over the pork and then pour 2 cups vinegar sauce over the top. Place the lid on the Dutch oven and cook 30 minutes over medium-high heat.

4. Preheat the oven to 350°.

5. Transfer the covered Dutch oven to the center rack of the oven. Cook slowly for 2 to 3 hours, depending on the size of the pork butt, until a meat thermometer inserted into the thickest portion registers 190° to 200°. The meat should be very tender and ready to be pulled apart. If there is a bone in the meat, it should come out smooth and clean, with no meat clinging to it (this is the real test for doneness on the barbecue circuit). Remember, there is no need to turn the meat during the entire cooking time.

6. At this point, the pork can be cooled in the Dutch oven and refrigerated overnight, if desired. (The advantage of doing this is that the extra fat will congeal and it will be very easy to lift off the top, leaving only the concentrated juices. Reheat the pork in the Dutch oven in a preheated 250° oven until hot all the way through; spoon the juices over the pork as it reheats, and then follow the rest of the instructions.)

7. Let the meat stand 20 minutes until cool enough to handle; wearing rubber food-service gloves, pull the meat from the skin, bones, and fat. Set aside any crispy bits. Working quickly, shred meat using two forks. (You can chop the meat with a cleaver if you prefer, but then you have "chopped" pork barbecue, not "pulled" pork.) Chop the reserved crispy bits and stir them into the pulled pork. While the meat is still warm, stir in about $^3/_4$ cup of the remaining vinegar sauce (depending on the meat) to moisten and season the meat. The recipe can be made in advance up to this point and reheated with about $^1/_4$ cup additional sauce in a double boiler or in a covered pan in a 250° oven.

8. Serve the pulled pork on buns topped with North Carolina Coleslaw. Serve additional sauce on the side, if desired.

NORTH CAROLINA VINEGAR SAUCE

makes about 6 cups

4 cups cider vinegar
1 cup ketchup
2 tablespoons kosher salt
2 tablespoons ground white pepper
½ to 1 tablespoon red pepper flakes
¼ cup granulated sugar
½ cup firmly packed brown sugar
1 teaspoon freshly ground black pepper

1. Combine all the ingredients in a large bowl and stir well. Let stand at least 10 minutes or almost indefinitely in the refrigerator. The longer the sauce stands, the hotter it gets because the heat from the red pepper is brought out by the vinegar. Start with ½ tablespoon red pepper and add more to taste.

NORTH CAROLINA COLESLAW

serves 8

3 cups North Carolina Vinegar Sauce or as needed
1 medium head green cabbage, cored and chopped

1. Combine the sauce and cabbage in a medium bowl and stir until the cabbage is well coated with sauce but not quite wet. Let stand 2 hours or overnight in the refrigerator.

PAN-ROASTED SAUSAGE, POTATOES, AND GRAPES

serves 4

Grapes and sausage may seem like an odd combination, but you'll love this satisfying dish from award-winning cookbook author Clifford A. Wright. The sweetness of the grapes acts as a wonderful foil for the spiciness of the hot sausage and red pepper. Be sure to cook this dish over low heat the entire time. Add a green salad and you've got dinner.

6 tablespoons extra-virgin olive oil

2 large garlic cloves, crushed

$3^{1}/_{2}$ pounds potatoes, cut into small cubes and dried well with paper towels

Salt

1 ($^{1}/_{2}$-pound) link sweet Italian sausage, casing removed and meat crumbled into small pieces

2 ($^{1}/_{2}$-pound) links hot Italian sausage, casings removed and meat crumbled into small pieces

1 teaspoon red pepper flakes (preferably Chimayo chile flakes)

$2^{1}/_{2}$ cups seedless green grapes (about $1^{1}/_{4}$ pounds)

Freshly ground black pepper

1. Heat the oil and garlic in a 12-or 14-inch cast iron skillet over low heat. Once the garlic turns light golden, remove and discard it.

2. Add the potatoes and shake the skillet so they cover the bottom. Salt lightly to taste. Place both kinds of sausage on top of the potatoes, sprinkle with the red pepper and cook until the potatoes are sticking and golden on the bottom, about 15 minutes.

3. Turn the mixture by scraping with a metal spatula and cook,

stirring occasionally, until golden brown, about 1 hour.

4. Add the grapes, season with salt and black pepper to taste, and cook until the grapes are soft, about 20 minutes. Serve hot.

PIMIENTO CHEESE PANINI SANDWICH

makes 1 sandwich

Nothing is simpler to make for a quick dinner than a delicious sandwich served with a salad or a bowl of soup. In this recipe, Gourmet Gadget Gal cooking instructor, food writer, and blogger Jane Gaither twists together two classic Southern sandwiches, the pimiento cheese and the BLT, and presses them into an oozy melt sure to please your family. If you don't own a panini press, you can always use a smaller preheated cast iron skillet to press the sandwich down. This recipe makes enough pimiento cheese for eight sandwiches and it will keep in your refrigerator for up to two weeks.

Pimiento Cheese Spread:
3   cups (12 ounces) shredded Cheddar cheese
1   (4-ounce) jar diced pimiento, drained
$1/2$ teaspoon minced garlic
1   teaspoon prepared horseradish
1   teaspoon hot sauce
1   teaspoon Worcestershire sauce
A few grinds of black pepper
6   tablespoons mayonnaise (Jane likes to use Duke's)
Panini:
Softened butter
2   ($1/3$-inch-thick) bread slices cut from a dense loaf
2   thick bacon slices (Jane uses Benton's from Madisonville, Tennessee), cooked until crisp

1   tomato, sliced

1. Combine the Pimiento Cheese Spread ingredients in a medium bowl and stir well.

2. Spread butter on one side of each bread slice.

3. Heat a 12-inch Lodge Grill Pan and Panini Press over medium-high heat.

4. Place 1 bread slice, buttered side down, on the hot grill pan. Spoon 3 tablespoons of the Pimiento Cheese Spread onto the bread and spread it to the edges. Add the bacon and sliced tomato and top with the second bread slice with the buttered side up.

5. Place the hot panini press on top of the sandwich for 2 minutes, pressing gently to flatten it.

6. Remove the press and transfer the sandwich to a plate. Enjoy!

Our Part 4 is here:

Michael Firsttest

The GREATEST LODGE
CAST IRON
Cookbook
Simple and Easy with
Over 150 Recipes for Your Cast-Iron Cookware

BOOK 4

Made in the USA
Monee, IL
03 July 2025

20460235R00055